Gray Whales

ABDO
Publishing Company

A Buddy Book
by
Julie Murray

VISIT US AT
www.abdopub.com

Published by Buddy Books, an imprint of ABDO Publishing Company, 4940 Viking Drive, Suite 622, Edina, Minnesota 55435. Copyright © 2005 by Abdo Consulting Group, Inc. International copyrights reserved in all countries. No part of this book may be reproduced in any form without written permission from the publisher.

Printed in the United States.

Edited by: Christy DeVillier
Contributing Editors: Matt Ray, Michael P. Goecke
Graphic Design: Maria Hosley
Image Research: Deborah Coldiron
Photographs: Corbis, Corel, Digital Vision, Minden Pictures, Photodisc

Library of Congress Cataloging-in-Publication Data

Murray, Julie, 1969-
  Gray whales / Julie Murray.
      p. cm. — (Animal kingdom)
  Summary: An introduction to the history, physical characteristics, and behavior of the gray whale, a toothless mammal of the northern Pacific Ocean.
  Includes bibliographical references (p.) and index.
  ISBN 1-59197-318-X
    1. Gray whale—Juvenile literature. [1. Gray whale. 2. Whales.] I. Title.

QL737.C425M87 2004
599.5'22—dc22
                                                              2003057883

Contents

Whales Are Cetaceans

What do whales, dolphins, and porpoises have in common? These animals are **cetaceans**. Cetaceans are **mammals** that live in the water.

Dolphins are mammals that live in the water.

Gray whales and other mammals have lungs for breathing.

Sea **mammals** are very different from fish. Fish have gills for breathing under water. Instead of gills, mammals use lungs for breathing air. Whales and all other mammals cannot breathe under water like fish.

Mammals are born alive instead of hatching from eggs. Baby mammals drink their mother's milk. Some mammals that live on land are elephants, apes, dogs, and mice. People are mammals, too.

Elephants are mammals that live on land.

Gray Whales

Gray whales are baleen whales.
Baleen whales do not have teeth. These
toothless whales have plates of string-
like baleen hanging inside their mouths.
They use their baleen to catch food.

These humpback whales are
using their baleen to catch food.

Gray whales are named for their grayish-looking skin. They often live in small groups called pods. A gray whale pod commonly has three or four members. Some pods have as many as 20 gray whales. Whales of different pods sometimes gather together to feed.

Dolphins, gray whales, and other whales **breach**. A breaching whale leaps from the water. Then, it falls back down making a big splash.

A breaching gray whale.

No one is sure why whales **breach**. Maybe breaching helps whales remove pests from their skin. Whales may breach to warn others of danger. Maybe breaching is how whales "show off" to other whales.

What They Look Like

Gray whales are large animals. They grow to become about 50 feet (15 m) long. Adult gray whales may weigh more than 35 tons (32 t).

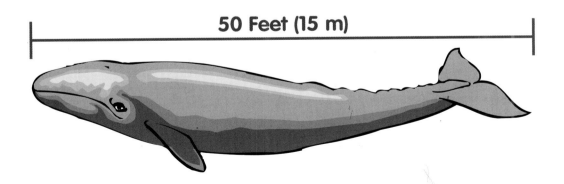

50 Feet (15 m)

Gray whales have dark skin with gray and white patches. They have a hump on their lower back. A line of ridges runs from their hump to their tail. The tail has two fins, or flukes, that jut out sideways.

A whale's tail fins are called flukes.

Whales use their flippers
for steering and balance.

The gray whale uses its big tail for swimming. It is about 10 feet (three m) across. Gray whales also have two **flippers**. These flippers are paddle-shaped and pointed on the tips.

Gray whales have two **blowholes** on the top of their head. They take in air and let it out through these holes. Water often leaks into the blowhole. The whale sprays out this water when it blows out air. The water can shoot more than 20 feet (six m) high.

This whale is blowing air out of its blowholes.

Barnacles

Some gray whales have barnacles living on their skin. Barnacles are small shellfish. They attach themselves to whales, ships, and other things. Barnacles may be orange, white, or yellow.

Barnacles attached to a gray whale.

Where They Live

Gray whales live in the Pacific Ocean. They **migrate** every year. Gray whales go to cold waters to eat. They go to warm waters to find mates and have babies.

A pod of migrating gray whales.

Some gray whales **migrate** between South Korea and the northern Siberian coast. Others migrate from the Chukchi and Bering Seas to Baja California, Mexico. It takes about three months to go each way. This is one of the longest migration trips of any **mammal**.

Eating

Gray whales eat amphipods. Amphipods are small shrimp-like animals.

Gray whales feed at the bottom of the ocean floor. They gulp a lot of food-filled water. The water escapes easily. But the food stays trapped among the baleen in their mouths.

Gray whales feed near the
ocean bottom.

Gray Whale Calves

Whale babies are called calves. Female gray whales have one calf at a time. They may have a calf every two to four years.

A gray whale and her calf.

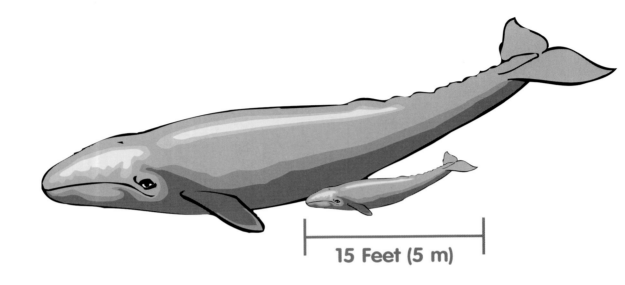

15 Feet (5 m)

A newborn gray whale calf is about 15 feet (five m). It may weigh as much as 1,500 pounds (680 kg). The calf stays close to its mother and drinks her milk. Gray whales may live to be 60 years old.

Important Words

blowhole the opening on top of a whale that is used for taking in air.

breaching when whales or dolphins leap from the water and fall down with a great splash.

cetacean a water mammal that has flippers, a tail, and one or two blowholes.

flipper a flat, paddle-shaped body part that cetaceans use to swim.

mammal most living things that belong to this special group have hair, give birth to live babies, and make milk to feed their babies.

migrate to move from one place to another when the seasons change.

Web Sites

To learn more about gray whales, visit ABDO Publishing Company on the World Wide Web. Web sites about gray whales are featured on our Book Links page. These links are routinely monitored and updated to provide the most current information available.

www.abdopub.com

Index